HOW TO EARN PASSIVE INCOME

BUSINESS SKILLS FOR EDITORS: 5

Louise Harnby

ISBN: 9798657636673

CONTENTS

Introduction

The problem with editing

Working with words is a wonderful way to earn a living but the nature of our business means the degree to which we can expand, or scale, is restricted. Anyone running an editing business runs up against two related problems. Here's the bottom line:

- Editing is a one-to-one transaction
- There are a fixed number of hours in a day

Editing is a one-to-one exchange of the client's money for our time. We edit and we get paid. If we want to get paid some more, we must edit some more. Running an editing business can therefore feel like being on a treadmill. We must continually push forward to keep the wheels turning.

Furthermore, because there are only so many hours in a day, no matter how fast we work, how efficiently we work, there will come a point when time runs out.

Any scaling of editing income requires one of three approaches:

- Putting in more hours so that we get more done in more time
- Increasing productivity so that we get more done in the same time
- Increasing our prices

All three approaches are valid and every editor would do well to consider the second two on at least an annual basis. However, they don't solve the problem long term.

We can put in more hours, but there are only 24 hours in a day, and only so many that can be set aside for editing. We're also restricted by the amount of time we can concentrate for without compromising on quality, such that even if we find additional hours, we might not be able to use them.

How about introducing efficiencies into our practice to help with the productivity problem? Even editors who've explored productivity measures fully will discover a baseline speed beyond which they can no longer work effectively.

And what of fee increases? Editors don't always set the price. Those who work primarily with publishers and packagers know this only too well. We can and should negotiate, but those organizations have profit margins to consider, just as we do. Price setting isn't something we necessarily have full control over.

Time *out* of our business

Every editor needs to take time out of their business.

Salaried employees (usually) have benefits attached to their contracts of employment such that they are paid when absent as a result of public holidays, annual leave, and bereavement, illness and family crises. Many employers allow for a certain number of days off a week, and for a set number of hours to be worked per workday. That means that time out of the business doesn't affect the employee's bank account.

That's not the case for independent editors. Time out means we're not editing, and since our earnings are based on a service transaction, that means no income.

Furthermore, editors can be forced to take time out for external reasons they have no control over. When client work dries up because the supply chain is interrupted – as some editors experienced during the COVID-19 pandemic – so does the income attached to it.

Time *on* our business

Every minute we spend on activities we do *for* our businesses – sales, marketing, quoting, training, continuing professional development, networking, invoicing, completing tax returns, tracking our data – are critical yet unbillable.

Yes, they drive income indirectly because they are the tools through which we acquire new and better-paying clients, secure the monies we're owed, and fulfil our legal obligations to the state. But no one actually pays us to find clients, declare our earnings or expand our skillset. In fact, there will be a *cost* to us – certainly our time, sometimes our money.

Light beyond the treadmill: Passive income

Still, there is light beyond the treadmill, and it is to be found in passive income.

Passive income is a different ballgame. It is the key to editorial business scalability because while it does require a lot of hard work initially – certainly time, perhaps even a little money – it too has a bottom line: once the product has been created, it will continue to earn us an income with no participation.

Unlike editing, which is a one-to-one transaction, passive income products (or PIPs) are one-to-many. And therein lies the opportunity.

The PIP Development Framework

In this guide, we'll start by looking at the advantages of having a passive-income stream – of which income is one. Then we'll get into the nitty-gritty with this guide's core tool: the PIP Development Framework.

The framework is a five-stage process that will help any editor explore the possibilities and develop their own PIP:

1. The solutions to problems and why they're at the core of passive-income opportunities
2. The audience
3. The shape of the content (including format, and how customers will access and pay for it)
4. The tools required to create the product
5. The options for promotion and visibility

There's also a short chapter about impostor syndrome and some ideas for how to manage it. I've included that because this is something that holds a lot of editors back and I don't want it to stop you, not least because by the time you've finished reading and working through this guide, it's my aim that you'll have a ready-to-go plan for your very own PIP, perhaps even more than one. Let's get going!

FOR YOU TO DO

The first step is to get your workbook ready – the **PIP planner**. You can make your own or copy or extract the one at the back of this guide. The planner is where you'll record your ideas and discoveries. Nothing is set in stone – you can add, revise or delete at any time.

Passive income: Definition and benefits

Defining passive income

Passive income is money earned from a product that doesn't require our active participation.

The core characteristics of a PIP

Good candidates for PIPs have several core characteristics:

- They are in demand
- They solve a problem
- They add a deeper level of value
- They are non-participatory one-to-many

Demand

A PIP must be in demand if it is to generate sales. It might sound like such an obvious thing to state but small business owners can fall foul of confusing their own passions and preferences for customers' and clients' requirements. And that's not the way to go when we want to maximize our passive income.

Example

In 2013, I wrote a book called *Business Planning for Editorial Freelancers*. It was my first book and a steep learning curve. I published it in ebook-only format because at the time I was in love with my new Kindle and reading everything digitally. Print books were a thing of the past! I would declutter my bookshelves, relish the white space on my walls, and never run out of something to read while travelling.

That was *my* preference. And that's where I came unstuck, because I assumed it was my readership's too. And even if it wasn't, I reasoned, if they wanted it badly enough, they'd put up with its being in a format they didn't want.

Sure enough, some did. But a surprising (to me, at least) number of people got in touch to ask when the paperback would be out because they wanted that or nothing.

Honestly, I didn't want to create a paperback at the time. Getting the ebook to market had been a lot of work and I was a little burned out. The thought of reformatting for print felt like a chore. And yet I was losing out on sales. If I'd researched what my core customer base preferred beforehand, I would have organized my publishing process differently.

I took a break – a little time to re-energize – reviewed my strategy, and did some research. A few months later, the print version was born.

The success of that book required my shifting away from a personal-preference mindset and focusing on a customer-demand one. And I will never again make the mistake of confusing my preferences for those of my customers because there is twice as much demand for print editions of my books as digital. That has nothing to do with my preferences; it's just a fact I must acknowledge.

If material lends itself well to a written format, and it's financially viable to offer it in print format, I'll do it because satisfying demand is the key to getting the most out of a passive income stream.

Problem-solving

A PIP should solve a perpetual problem, because where there's a perpetual problem there's a perpetual demand for solutions.

Everyone has problems because no one knows everything. Editors want to learn, and so do our clients.

Let's divide up the knowledge people have about all the stuff there is to know into three broad categories:

- Most people know nothing about some things
- Most people know a little about many things
- Most people know lot about a few things

It's that final category – a lot about a few – where the opportunities for PIPs lie. That's because it's likely that each of us knows a lot about a few things that others don't but wish they did.

People's time is limited and although there's a lot of superb free stuff available on Google, it's often first-step rather than deep-dive information – a glimpse at a solution. Or perhaps there's a blog, vlog or podcast with loads of useful information on it but it requires a lot of effort to navigate that content.

When we go that extra step and provide comprehensive solutions to problems in an accessible structured one-stop-shop format – frameworks, paradigms, step-by-step how-to learning – we can charge for that because of the added value we're providing.

Example

Over the course of several years, a social science editor has written thirty blog posts about various aspects of thesis writing. They're all excellent articles but the fact that they've been published on a biweekly blog means they're not structured in a logical format that would take a graduate student from point A to point B.

The blog content drives student traffic to the editor's website and generates leads for editing work. But what if the editor repurposed that content into a 20,000-word guide that offered that logical framework, a one-stop shop to getting it right, and sold it via their website?

That's a great example of a product that would solve problems and generate passive income for our editor.

Deep added value

A PIP must add a deeper level of value. A product that promises a solution but doesn't deliver will generate requests for refunds and negative reviews rather than glowing testimonials and recommendations.

Quality comes in the form of the deep-dive, the one-stop shop, the journey from A to B. That's what allows the customer to move beyond glimpses. Instead, they can acquire knowledge and/or skills such that they're able to do something they couldn't previously.

Example

There's plenty of opinion in editing forums about what to charge. There are plenty of free blog posts that discuss rates (I've written some myself). But what some editors want is to cut through the noise.

The Chartered Institute of Editing and Proofreading's guide *Pricing a Project: How to prepare a professional quotation* by editor Melanie Thompson is a great example of a PIP that solves a recognized problem but goes the extra mile by offering readers a step-by-step pricing framework, one that helps them understand the process, the factors that influence it, and the market they're operating in. It's no glimpse. It's not an opinion piece. It's a compact deep-dive tool that, once read, enables editors to act. That's why it sells so well and why it's in its second edition.

Non-participatory one-to-many

Editing is one-to-one active participation – we create one product (the edited file) one time and sell it (via our fee) one time to the one client who commissioned us. Any additional projects, even for the same client, require fresh input. We agree a fee and get paid for *doing* something – editing or proofreading their material. No doing means no income.

There are one-to-many income opportunities for editors that also require *doing* something each time. Examples include:

- Running training workshops and seminars
- Hosting live webinars
- Paid speaking engagements

These aren't PIPs because the editor must still engage, even if some of the materials required need only be created once. Although the income is welcome and valuable, it must be earned each time.

But one-to-many products *can* be PIPs – we create one product one time and sell it to lots of different people – but we do so without having to participate.

Examples

Here are two examples of the different approaches to one-to-many income sources – one participatory, one not.

1: The assessed course

Sophie Playle of Liminal Pages runs a six-week fiction-editing course called 'Tea and Commas: The Foundations of Line and Copy-Editing Fiction'. Students must register for limited places when the course opens. The course comprises a series of PDF modules that are sent on a weekly basis. These include assignments on which students receive personalized feedback.

This is *not* a PIP because the course is guided – Sophie must participate, and the price rightly reflects that.

2: The self-directed course

I offer a multimedia fiction-editing course called 'Switching to Fiction'. There is no fixed registration period – students can buy it whenever they wish and are granted lifetime access to the materials 24/7. The course comprises a webinar, a book, and supporting resources including a style-sheet template and a sample report.

This *is* a PIP because the course is self-guided – I don't participate in the students' learning, and the price reflects that.

The benefits of PIPs

Now we know what makes a passive income stream distinctive, let's look at some of the benefits.

Increasing recurring income

The first benefit of a PIP is the obvious one: it increases our earnings. Still, it's worth acknowledging because PIPs offer us the opportunity to scale our income in a way that editing can't – they're one-to-many products that don't require participation.

One of the most-oft discussions raised in online editing forums is rates. Of course, we can set our own rates when we're dealing directly with the client. But if we're an editor who sources their work primarily from third parties such as publishers, packagers, and project-management agencies, we won't have full control over the pricing process.

Many editors like these types of clients precisely because they do all the client-acquisition work, whereas those of us who work directly with clients have to do our own marketing.

And so it might be that an editor wants to continue to work with their publisher clients, enjoys the work, feels fulfilled by it. And yet they're unable to negotiate a rate increase or add more hours into their schedule.

PIPs provide supplementary income without requiring us to increase the time we commit to our business, nor dilute the hours we already have.

How much extra income, you might ask? It depends on what you charge, how many you sell, how visible your PIP is, the degree to which you've satisfied a demand that isn't being supplied, the degree to which you can access the target audience, and their trust in you. We'll look more at these issues in the PIP Development Framework modules.

Evergreen product; recurring income

Because PIPs solve perpetual problems, their content is evergreen, meaning they won't go out of date the day after you've created them.

No one can guarantee that some kind of change won't affect the demand for a product over time. Technology is possibly the driver of change most likely to affect a PIP's lifespan. I don't sell my digital proofreading stamps, but if I did and PDFs became a thing of the past, the stamps would go with them. That's worth considering during the planning stage.

However, the kinds of PIPs editors will be creating are likely to have longevity, which means the income stream has longevity too. Yes, the initial work is hard, but it's a one-off exercise; and the income is a recurring benefit.

A marketing tool that positions you as an expert

PIPs aren't free but they're problem-solving content all the same. And good content shows rather than tells of expertise.

- Editing websites with lists of qualifications say to the visitor: *Look at me – I'm great.*
- Editing websites with lots of useful problem-solving content say to the visitor: *I'm looking at you. I can help **you** be great.*

When a client or a colleague has a problem, and you have a solution, that demonstrates expertise and inspires trust. And so while you might sell your PIP to that person, you might also sell editing services to them (if they're a potential client) or receive referrals from them (if they're a colleague).

Your PIP is therefore a marketing tool as well as a source of additional income because it positions you as a generous expert.

Creating a buffer for our editing business

Another topic that's frequently discussed among editors is how full the client cupboard is.

There is no true certainty in the world of freelance editing. Publisher clients can merge with other presses and streamline their freelance lists; packager schedules can change because an author hasn't delivered the files; students have long holidays; enthusiastic indie authors transform into silent no-shows; and global pandemics shut down some supply chains.

All of which means that editors, particularly those who loathe marketing, are at best affected by seasonal variation and at worst vulnerable in a market they have little control over.

PIPs act as a growth tool when our schedules are full, a buffer when leads are slow, and a lifeline when the cupboard is bare.

Something for the client who's not ready to invest

Not every potential client will be ready to invest in editing. Depending on the nature of the project, they could be looking at spending hundreds or thousands of pounds (or whatever your local currency is). However, they might be ready to buy a PIP, especially if the price is relatively small in comparison to the edit.

And that's where the deep added value comes into play. If your PIP can offer expert solutions that will help drive the customer forward for a price that's affordable – regardless of the season, the health of the world population, and any other myriad obstacles – it will sell better and earn you more income.

FOR YOU TO DO

I mentioned how creating passive-income streams requires an initial investment of our time. I recommend you give some thought to how you will **make time** for the planning and creation of your PIP. There's no one true way. Some like lots of short sprints; others prefer the middle distance – chunks of hours each week; yet others prefer the marathon and go all out until it's done. Much will depend on your lifestyle and work commitments – do what suits you best.

Stage 1: What problems can you solve?

What do you know?

Problems are the foundation to a great PIP because that's what we solve. Still, we need the skills, knowledge and experience to solve them if we're going to create something that helps people so much that they'll pay for it.

All of us know stuff – not just in the world of words, but beyond. Some of our clients and colleagues will wish they knew that stuff too. A good first place to start is to think about what you know, what you're already good at. Think about the following:

- The type of editorial service(s) you offer (e.g. developmental editing, line editing, copyediting, proofreading, beta reading, sensitivity reading, formatting, indexing, layout and design)
- Your niche specialisms and sub-specialisms (e.g. crime fiction, veterinary medicine, engineering, romance, business, corporate comms, post-apocalyptic zombie fiction)
- Your strengths as a business owner (e.g. time management, productivity, finance, knowledge of Wordpress websites, SEO, IT, organizational skills, balancing work and life)
- Your educational and career background knowledge (e.g. physiotherapy, chemistry, political science, creative writing)

Those things, especially combinations of those things, mean you know what others don't, which in turn means you can solve their problems effectively and credibly.

Why problems matter

No one likes having problems. Content that solves them is therefore valuable, whether it's free or paid for.

People with problems are often time-poor. It takes time to find full solutions via all the wonderful free stuff available on the internet because that tends to be restricted to glimpses or tasters that solve only part of a problem.

One-stop-shop solutions – the deep dives – are therefore even more valuable. They don't just teach our customers what they want to know; they save them time too. That's why we can and should charge for that added value.

Broadly, there are three types of problems that are ripe for consideration:

1. Already solved, but not with your voice
2. Partially solved, but there are gaps
3. Those for which there are no existing solutions

Solutions to problems (2) and (3) are easier to sell but (1) must not be discounted for reasons I discuss below.

1. The problem has been solved, but not with your voice

Those who aren't used to creating content often worry that they'll be wasting their time because the content already exists in some form or another. Why write another recipe book when lots already exist? Why build another smartphone when lots already exist? Why write another book about self-editing when many editing books have already been published?

Here are some ideas to help you reframe your focus.

Who's interested in you?

You're the only you, which makes you interesting because you'll have a personal angle on the solution that brings a fresh voice to the table.

You also have genre/subject specialisms and editing experience that might bring a particular flavour to your PIP's content.

Furthermore, if someone's landed on your website or found you in a directory, they already have their hand at least partially raised, which means they're interested in what *you* think. Why not show them?

What will the PIP say about you?

Recall the earlier discussion about showing versus telling. Even if there are already products being sold that tackle the same problems, they're not showing your colleagues and clients that *you* have, or understand, the solutions, which means they're not working to garner trust for you; nor are they positioning you as the expert.

That, along with your voice, means there's space to consider a PIP.

Example

In 2020, technical writer John Espirian published a book called *Content DNA*. Is he the first person to write a book about content and branding? No, he is not. There are tons of books on the subject. I myself have produced guides on content marketing and branding – they're part of my Business Skills for Editors series, along with this guide on passive income.

However, John's book is distinct from my guides and every other book about content marketing for the following reasons:

- It's written by John, and there's only one John, which means it has his voice and perspective.

- The framework in which he helps readers understand content and branding is that of 'the shape of your business'. It's a distinct approach that helps people visualize the concepts he discusses.
- John considers this a marketing tool as much as anything else. His day job requires him to write clear on-brand copy for B2B clients with big budgets and even bigger reputations to protect. *Content DNA* helps him show them that he's up to the job, that he understands their problems, and has the skills to offer superb solutions.
- John already has a huge following on LinkedIn, something he's built using the strategy he covers in the book but also in another PIP he offers: 'How not to be a LinkedIn Loser', a 3-part pre-recorded video series he sells for £69. That means he has an audience of hand-raisers who are interested in his solutions.

2. The problem has been partially solved, but there are gaps

An alternative is to consider the spaces *in between* the existing content. That's been my own approach. The market is rammed with broad guidance, but editors can find gaps by focusing on specialist audiences, niche topics, and alternative formats. And when we create PIPs that combine those three elements, the offering is even more compelling.

Specialist audience

Imagine a problem that you know how to solve – for example, you can help clients create style guides so that their internal communications are consistent and on-brand. The CIEP has a guide called *Your House Style*, which is suitable for just about any reader. However, can you use your specialist knowledge or career background to create a PIP that solves the same problem specifically for a specialist audience? Health centres, engineering companies, physiotherapy practices, schools and colleges, property companies could be examples.

Those niche audiences have their own language, and if you're fluent in more than one of them there's nothing to stop you creating more than one PIP. You wouldn't have to start from scratch each time either; you could repurpose the original content and reframe it for the relevant niche market.

Niche topics

Think also about a niche focus. Story-level fiction editors often find the same problems arising in their client work – a lack of suspense and flat characterization, for example. Non-fiction editors often come across problems with structure and inappropriate tone of voice. PIPs that focus on solving those niche problems rather than offering broad-brush writing guidance can be compelling.

Alternative formats

People have different preferences when it comes to learning. Some like audiovisual content supported with written materials. Others like to sit in a classroom. Others want a live webinar. Yet others prefer to be self-guided with written-only materials. If there's a problem you know how to solve but it's already been solved in one format – a classroom course, for example – might you create your own teaching in an alternative format?

Examples

1. The specialist audience

The market is awash with books about marketing for small businesses. What it is not awash with is books about marketing for editorial business owners. Which is why I wrote *Marketing Your Editing & Proofreading Business*. First published back in 2014, it continues to be one of my most popular books. It's for editors and only editors. Not dentists or builders or hairdressers. Just editors!

In 2020, editor Maya Berger launched The Editor's Affairs – a customizable Excel-based tool that offers editors a no-fuss way to log, track, review and analyse their data so that they understand the health of their business. It speaks our language; it's built to accommodate our client types; it's just for us. Not dentists, builders or hairdressers!

2. The niche topic

There are several established courses for editors wishing to learn how to be a fiction editor. However, I saw a gap in the market – something that would enable non-fiction editors to learn what gaps they'd need to fill in their *existing* knowledge base if they were to move into fiction editing. My online multimedia course 'Switching to Fiction' solved that problem, and I priced it such that it would be affordable to those who weren't yet ready to commit to an intensive programme of fiction-focused learning.

3. The alternative format

The CIEP has an online course called 'Proofreading Theses and Dissertations'. It costs over a hundred pounds. It's a great course and will suit some students perfectly. However, the Institute recognizes that some people want a comprehensive written form of that content. *Proofreading Theses and Dissertations* is the solution. It's a written guide that costs a tenth of the price and offers an alternative way of accessing some of the core learning modules from the course.

3. No one has solved the problem

The final option is to develop a PIP that solves a problem for which, to your knowledge, there's no existing solution. This is the hardest but the most exciting route to take. It's likely that the problem will be niche, which is fine; niche is where much of the opportunity for PIPs lies.

Perhaps you regularly come up against a problem in your working day that slows you down and frustrates you. Have you already found a solution? If not, could you? And if you have or you could, might you teach others how to solve that problem too? If you can, there's a PIP waiting for you!

19

Or perhaps you offer a niche service but have noticed that there's no training available via the established training providers.

Example

I found writing comprehensive editorial reports for my fiction clients a huge frustration – it was laborious and time-consuming. I'm a line editor, so I'm paid to fix (or suggest fixes for) poor line craft. Still, I want my clients to understand the *why* of my edits so that they don't bombard me with queries and because a comprehensive report helps them develop their writing skills.

The solution came in the form of a detailed, branded template with pre-written explanations of various aspects of line craft. It saved me hours and hours. I thought it would save my fellow editors hours and hours, too. So I created a multimedia course called 'How to Write the Perfect Fiction Editorial Report'. It includes the template, an ebook, two sample reports, and a tracking checklist. It's been a success because there's nothing else like it.

Where to find problem-focused inspiration

Problems that inspire and underpin our PIPs manifest in multiple ways:

- Editing forums
- Client work
- Client reports
- Our email inboxes
- Social media direct-messaging platforms
- In our own heads
- Conventions and other networking events
- Training courses and workshops
- Business deficiencies in our practice

- Existing problem-solving content we've already made available for free via, for example, a blog, podcast or YouTube channel

Examples

Over the course of a couple of years, authors and editors emailed me to say they loved the content I post on The Editing Blog about line craft but wished it were available in book form. So I wrote that book: *Editing Fiction at Sentence Level*.

I also read numerous threads in online editing forums in which editors said they wanted to blog but had no idea how to do it well. I developed a multimedia online course called 'Blogging for Business Growth' and a shorter guide called *How to Build an Editorial Blog*.

Your PIP: Starting afresh or repurposing?

Whether you build your PIP from scratch or repurpose existing content will depend largely on what you've been up to. There is absolutely nothing wrong with repurposing existing free content to generate a paid-for product as long as it solves a problem, adds value, and has an audience. If you own the copyright on your content, it's yours to do with as you wish.

Look back at the list above and think about who you've written for, who you've talked to, who you've stood up in front of, and what materials you created to communicate your message. That's the stuff of repurposing magic. It's yours, it probably took you a long time to put together, and you are entitled to develop it and sell it.

Example

You run a 1.5-hour workshop for twenty editors on sensitivity reading at your editorial society's annual convention. You're not paid for this gig – it's a free service to your community. You spend weeks preparing the content: slides, worksheets, a resource list, and a 10-page A4 study guide that delegates can take away with them.

You attend the meeting and the workshop goes swimmingly. You receive excellent feedback from the convention manager, feel a warm glow as you're invited to participate in next year's event, and drop your slides, worksheets, resource list and study guide into a corner and focus on meeting your next client's deadline. That novel won't edit itself.

… And then you pick the whole lot up and take a second look, because valuable stuff shouldn't be given away for free to twenty people and then abandoned! It can be developed and sold to an audience beyond the twenty people who spoke so highly of you to the convention manager.

You do the following:

- **Review the slides:** The draft slide deck contains a lot of valuable content that you had to omit from the workshop owing to time restrictions. You can add that back in.
- **Add audio:** You check out PowerPoint's within-slide audio tool to record a voiceover.
- **Create a video:** You save the content, including the audio, as an MP4. Now your slide deck is a pre-recorded training webinar.
- **Redesign the study guide:** Your ten pages of A4 aren't pretty – you wanted to save trees so squashed as much as you could into the space available. Again, there's valuable draft content that had to be omitted. You add it back in, revise the whole file, redesign the layout and arrange for it to be professionally proofread. Now it's an 8x5-inch ebook. All you need is a cover.
- **Revise the worksheets:** You review and revise the worksheets so that they reflect the additional draft content.

- **Branding:** The video, study guide, resource list and worksheets need branding so that the whole package is identifiable as a product in itself, and as something from your editing studio. You head for Canva and get creative.
- **Reviews:** You ask the twenty editors who attended the session whether they'd consider giving you a testimonial.
- **The launch:** You create a secret page on your website and add all the content for 'An Introduction to Sensitivity Reading' to your website. Then you get busy with your promotion strategy.

From service-to-community to sale

We can turn our existing content into masterclasses, the value of which can be experienced by an audience beyond those who accessed the original pared-down version.

And we know the content has value because we've been told so by those whose opinions we trust – people who've read our blogs, attended our seminars and workshops, invited us to speak, and asked to shake our hand because we helped them. That's the best place to start with a great PIP!

FOR YOU TO DO

Access your planner and go to the section on **problems, skills and solutions**. Make notes about the following:

What are you good at and what do you know?

Record your specialist skills – not just the editorial ones:

- The type(s) of editing you offer
- Your niche specialisms and sub-specialisms
- Your strengths as a business owner
- Your background knowledge

What problems do you encounter?

Make a note of the problems you regularly solve:

- In your client work
- In your networking and training spaces
- In your head
- In your business processes

What PIP(s) can you create that will fill the gaps?

Assess the existing sources of knowledge available against what you can bring to the table. Focus on the three types of problems discussed earlier and record your ideas for PIPs in relation to the following:

- Your angle and position in the market
- Niche approaches and new formats
- Gaps you can take advantage of

What content do you already have?

Make a note of all the content you've created and received great feedback on. Dig it out of the corner (or wherever it is) and think about how that can be developed into a PIP. Sources might include the following:

- The conventions you've spoken at
- The training you've done
- The content you've written and published anywhere

Stage 2: Focusing on audience

Why audience matters

Now that you have your initial ideas for PIPs, it's time to think about audience. Audience matters because without one we have no one to sell our PIP to, which means our passive income product is reduced to just a product – which is a waste of time.

Potential audiences

Think about the problems we discussed in the previous chapter, and the notes you made in your planner. Who has those problems? Is it one of the following, or something else?:

- Indie fiction authors – new, emerging, developed
- Indie non-fiction authors – new, emerging, developed
- Students – undergrad, postgrad or doctoral
- Academics – by specialism
- Scientists
- Educators
- Freelance editors and proofreaders – by specialism
- Contractors
- Publishing services agencies
- In-house editors
- Small business owners – by specialism
- Big corporates
- Government organizations
- Charities, NGOs, quangos

Does your audience know and trust you?

Having a great PIP will not help you increase income if you can't get it in front of your target audience. They need to know you and *trust* you.

Trust is important because you're asking for money. The audience for your PIP needs to believe their hard-earned cash will be well spent on the added value you're offering. Given that the editing market globally is unregulated – anyone can start an editorial business; anyone can call themselves a professional editor – telling them we're trustworthy is not enough; we need to show it too.

It's true that PIPs in themselves are part of that engagement strategy – that expert positioning I mentioned in the section on the benefits of PIPs – but when that's backed up by other indicators, trust will build much, much faster.

How does your introductory message make people feel?

Who are we most likely to hand over our money to? A friend or a stranger? Business owners and brands work similarly. Imagine a space where your audience is hanging out. Think about the *first* words that come out of your mouth (or pixels you place on the screen):

- 'I have this great thing that will solve your problems and it costs £30.'
- 'I have this great thing that will solve your problems and it costs nothing.'

The first of the two statements above encourages a *transactional* relationship; the second encourages an *emotional* one. Emotional relationships are where trust comes from. It's customary to get to know people before we ask for something – that's the same in any walk of life. If you don't know people, *give* them stuff first (attention, a solution, encouragement etc.); it will evoke an emotional response in them.

Two ways to be helpful

There are two powerful ways to get helpful, free, problem-solving stuff that builds trust in front of an audience:

- Direct engagement
- Content marketing

If you're someone who regularly answers questions in forums and offers solutions to problems in a way that's generous and mindful, you're already great at building relationships and garnering trust. Keep at it. The disadvantage of this method is that it requires participation; you need to be present for it to work. Those who are present are always the ones who are top of mind when it comes to direct engagement.

Content marketing does the same thing – offers solutions to problems without asking for anything in return – but it works for you even when you're asleep. You can't schedule a conversation during snooze time; you can schedule a blog post on your website, a podcast on iTunes, and a video on YouTube.

Example

The stranger's strange app

You're an editor and a bit of a tech nerd. You're also really into the psychology of words and work for a lot of academics and science publishers in the field of behavioural science. Topics such as mental health, wellbeing, a healthy editing and writing mindset, and the intersection between mental health and technology fascinate you.

You come up with a solution to a problem that's never been solved – an app that makes impostor syndrome go away. You've tested and trialled and tweaked and transformed. And it works!

Your audience is editors, who, you suspect, form one of the most impostor-syndrome-riddled communities on the planet. You yourself were plagued by it until you developed ImpostorBuster. So plagued by it, in fact, that you don't interact with the online editing community and you've never been to your national society's annual conference.

But that's all about to change because now you are impostor-syndrome-free and ready to unveil your PIP to the world!

You head for the spaces where editors hang out – Facebook groups, Twitter, LinkedIn, society forums, annual conventions – and announce that they, too, can rid themselves of impostor syndrome. ImpostorBuster is usually £150 but for a limited time only you're offering a 50% discount.

ImpostorBuster? Really? It's a bold claim. Plus, no one knows who you are, never mind whether they can trust what you say. And so ImpostorBuster flops and all the editors with impostor syndrome carry on doubting their accomplishments, while at the same time doubting your claims.

The friend's game-changing app

In another dimension, where things are almost but not quite the same, you're still an editor, still a tech nerd, and still interested in behavioural science and the psychology of words. But here's something new – you're engaged.

You have a podcast called Mental Tech, and your website has loads of booklets and resources that help editors and writers manage their emotional wellbeing.

People know you and like you. You're a bit quirky and geek out about things that most people wouldn't think to geek out about, but you have this way of making that geekery accessible and engaging.

And so when you turn up in forums, on social media platforms, and in other online and face-to-face spaces where you're known and liked, and perceived as helpful and generous, people are happy to listen. When you tell your editing and writing pals about ImpostorBuster, they have a lot of questions about this PIP but they know you wouldn't make such a bold claim if you hadn't tested it. And so they take you up on your half-price offer.

Why? Because they're sick and tired of doubting themselves but they've never doubted you. That's because you've invested time in building an emotional relationship with them, via content that shows them your claims can be trusted.

Don't wait

Start your emotional-relationship-building journey with your audience now. Create valuable useful resources related to the problems you're good at solving.

The alternative is that you will be launching your PIP into a field of crickets. That's not how to earn passive income; that's how to spend time on something that no one will know about or buy.

There's nothing wrong with asking for help in networking spaces but in order to build trust such that people will buy from you, you must ensure your focus is on giving help, not taking it.

FOR YOU TO DO

Access your planner and go to the section on **audience**. Refer back to the section on problems and your ideas for PIPs. Make a note of the following:

- Who the audience is
- How you will access them
- Whether they know and trust you
- What you need to do to maintain or build trust

Then start engaging, either directly or with content. Ideally, your strategy will include both. Make a list of the related resources that you'll create to form the basis of a rich, shareable content library. You can use the same tactics that are addressed in the chapter on PIP promotion.

Stage 3: The shape of the content

The shape of your PIP

Once you've identified the PIP you want to create and the audience it's intended for, decisions need to be made about the type of product you'll offer to market, the format you'll offer it in, how your audience will access it, and how they'll pay for it.

Type of product

There could be multiple options available. Just as you might have repurposed existing free content (e.g. a workshop from a conference) to create your PIP, so you might create multiple versions of your PIP to satisfy different audiences' preferences.

Your PIP could be one of the following:

- A self-guided course
- A deep-dive study guide
- A book
- A tool

Format

There are multiple choices when it comes to format, and you could decide to offer some or all of the options with each PIP type. Here are some ideas:

- **Self-guided course:** Pre-recorded video (e.g. webinar), printable PDFs (e.g. book, ebook, workbook, checklist, samples), Word and/or Excel template, video tutorial, questions and model answers, audio material
- **Deep-dive study guide:** Print, ebook (EPUB, MOBI), PDF, audio book

- **Book:** Print, ebook (EPUB, MOBI), PDF, audio book
- **Tool:** Code, installation wizard, software template, widget, app

Multimedia courses

Multimedia courses that incorporate several different components are a strong offering because they allow the customer to discover the solutions to their problems in multiple ways and learn at their own pace.

Plus, some types of content work better in particular formats. For example, a Word or Excel template can be edited by the customer to suit their own needs; a written version of the audiovisual content can be accessed across multiple devices; a video helps customers visualize core learning points and enables you to demonstrate the use of particular tools.

Multimedia courses are time-consuming to create. However, there could be opportunities to scale. For example, you could take one valuable element out of the package and create a more affordable 'lite' offering for customers with different budgets and preferences.

Books and guides

Books and study guides are prime candidates for print and electronic formatting. As editors, we're used to working with words on hard copy and electronically, so creating this type of content is less likely to push us out of our comfort zone.

While it will be feasible to create print and electronic versions of lengthier books, a print version of the short-form study guide might not be viable for print-on-demand via the likes of Amazon KDP.

Self-publishing any length of book or guide beyond PDF can also be tricky when it comes to content with non-text elements such as tables, grids and images, all of which might require specialist formatting skills. If you don't have those skills, hiring a pro will add costs to your PIP creation, so do think about how you present your written content.

An alternative is to research the costs of bulk printing, but that means you'll have to handle delivery too. Time and money must be factored in because if you're only charging £6 for a study guide, the return on your investment might not be sufficient to warrant the work involved, even if that means you lose customers who will only buy the written word in hard copy.

Tools

Macros, widgets, plugins and apps are not something I have experience with. If you don't either, think carefully about the costs of development before you go down this route. Consider maintenance, in particular. The whole point of creating a PIP is to create an income stream that doesn't require your participation. If you end up spending time on maintaining the tool's functionality in an ever- and fast-changing digital world, you've defeated the point of the exercise.

Access

You'll need to decide how the customer will access the content. Again, there are multiple options and you need not restrict yourself to only one:

Self-guided courses

- Printed materials – hard copy mailed to student
- Digital and printable media – hosted on a restricted page on your website to which customer is given access
- Digital and printable media hosted on PDF – files delivered electronically to customer by you
- Digital and printable media hosted on a third-party ecommerce platform (e.g. Udemy, Hotmart, Payhip, Sellfy, Podia)

Study guides and books

- Print – hard copy mailed to customer by you
- Print – hard copy mailed to retailer (e.g. Amazon)
- Ebook – file delivered electronically to customer by you
- Ebook – file hosted by and delivered electronically to customer by retailer (e.g. Amazon, Payhip)
- Ebook – file hosted on a restricted page on your website to which customer is given access
- PDF – file delivered electronically to customer by you
- PDF – file hosted on a restricted page on your website to which customer is given access
- Audio book – file delivered electronically to customer by you
- Audio book – file hosted by and delivered electronically to customer by retailer (e.g. Amazon or Audible, Payhip)
- Audio book – file hosted on a restricted page on your website to which customer is given access

Tools

- Code – memory stick mailed to customer by you
- Code – delivered electronically to customer by you
- Code – file hosted on a restricted page on your website to which customer is given access
- Installation wizard – downloaded directly from your website
- Installation wizard – downloaded from a third-party website
- Software template – file delivered electronically to customer by you
- Software template – file hosted on a restricted page on your website to which customer is given access

Self-hosting versus third party

Digital self-hosting has its advantages. First, if you're hosting on your own website, you control the space so that the brand identity of the PIP matches that of the public pages surrounding it. Second, it brings customers to your land and keeps them there. That tells the search engine algorithms that your website is providing a good customer experience. Third, you can update your PIP's content easily, something that's not possible with printed products. Fourth, digital hosting means fast delivery. Your customer might live thousands of miles away, meaning heavy postage costs and lengthy supply times. And, fifth, you're not handing over a cut of your income to a third party.

Still, Amazon is the biggest bookstore on the planet. My view is that an editor would be bonkers not to at least test selling books and guides on that platform. Even if print isn't viable, an ebook will be. Third-party retailers reduce your passive income, but they reduce your workload too. That's a trade-off you might be willing to make. My preference is therefore to go wide – customers can buy PDFs of most of my books direct from me or they can head for Amazon.

Ecommerce platforms are a good option if the time you'd save on providing access to your products would justify the cut taken by the third party to manage delivery and payment on your behalf. For example, authorpreneur Joanna Penn uses Payhip to serve customers who want to buy direct from her. I recommend starting with self-hosting to maximize profit; review if it becomes cumbersome.

Payment

Finally, you'll need to decide how payment will be made. This will be determined in part by your access choices and your website's capability. Options include:

- Website store plugin
- Website order-form page with buttons that link to a third-party payment system (e.g. PayPal or Stripe)

- You invoice and the customer pays by direct bank transfer, cash or cheque
- Third-party retailer handles the transaction (e.g. Amazon, Payhip or Udemy)

Any third-party payment system (e.g. PayPal or Stripe) will take a cut. For many editors (including me), that's a price worth paying for the security and convenience offered. If your PIP does as well as I hope it will, you could end up spending valuable time on invoices and receipts. Having a PayPal button on your website takes away a lot of work and reduces your participation.

Furthermore, some electronic products are taxable (and at different rates depending on where your customer lives and what your national tax rules are). If Amazon or Udemy is hosting the product and handling the transaction, any additional costs will be managed by them (even if the impact is felt by you).

Cheques ensure the money comes straight to you but they're a pain! Even though online banking has made digital deposits possible, overseas cheques can be problematic. Furthermore, direct bank transfers are popular in some countries (e.g. the UK) but less favoured in others (e.g. the US). Bear this in mind when deciding what payment options to offer.

Your audience's preferences

It's likely that your audience will comprise people with multiple preferences. That's why repurposing PIPs into various types and formats can make sense. Some customers lap up audio content; some learn best with audiovisual; some are book lovers. There isn't one way of doing something that will satisfy everyone.

If you receive feedback from your audience that indicates opportunities for scaling up or down – either developing a shorter-form content into a multimedia PIP or paring down a multimedia offering into something smaller – embrace this market information. However, when deciding whether to go ahead, make sure you know where the value lies and price accordingly.

Examples

The course

My course 'How to Write the Perfect Fiction Editorial Report' comprises the following:

- a recorded webinar with subtitles/closed captions
- a PDF ebook containing the written version of the content
- case studies
- an editable editorial report template
- a clickable checklist to aid template navigation
- sample editorial reports
- two video tutorials
- a resource list of suggested line-craft books and links to macros and tools for fiction editors

A customer asked me if I'd do a pared-down version for a lower price that excluded the webinar, the resource list and the links. I declined for the following reasons:

- The webinar and the ebook are complements, not stand-alones. I offer both because some customers want to read and others want to watch and listen. Consequently, I don't charge more because I've offered two ways to access this information.
- The primary value is in the editable template and clickable checklist – these are the things everyone raves about and that save them oodles of time – is in the editable template and clickable checklist. There's still secondary value in the other components, but that's not where the vision of the PIP came from.

FOR YOU TO DO

Access your planner and go to the section on **shape**. Record your ideas about the following:

- What type of PIP suits your content best?
- Are there opportunities for scaling up or down?
- What formats will you offer it in?
- Will you self-host and/or use a third-party platform?
- What payment system(s) will you use?

Stage 4: Creation tools

Bringing the PIP to life

You've worked out the problems you want to solve and for whom, and you know what shape your PIP will take, at least in its initial form. Now it's time to bring it to life.

In this chapter we'll look at the kit you might need to create video, audio, and written content. There are many ways to create and host learning materials but I want this guide to be accessible to *any* editor. And so I've opted for tools that don't require a huge learning curve, are low cost (or even free), and that might well be sitting on your desktop already.

Creating written content

Written content is valuable because it's accessible. Even if you're creating videos, a written version of the material will provide students with something to refer back to as they work on their ideas.

Editors will already be aware of the various tools to create written content: Word, InDesign, Google Docs, Scrivener. Use whatever you feel comfortable with. My preference is Microsoft Word, for the following reasons:

- Most of us already own it
- We have a good understanding of its functionality
- Word files can be uploaded to Amazon KDP for ebooks
- PDFs can be uploaded to Amazon KDP for print books

If you're hosting written content on your website, and it doesn't need to be fully editable, turn it into a PDF.

Be mindful of the fonts you use. You might have downloaded beautiful fonts that aren't built into Word. That could mean that what your customer sees in the finished design isn't what you're looking at. You can embed fonts, though this can affect the degree to which you can optimize/compress your PDF.

Embedding fonts

To embed fonts in a Word document on PC, go to the File tab. Then choose Options>Save>Embed fonts in the file.

Creating PDFs

Use the save-as function to create a PDF from a Word document. You'll need a PDF editor. Adobe's free Reader does the basics very well but for optimization/compression and other jiggery-pokery, you'll need to upgrade to the full version of Acrobat.

PDF-XChange and PDFelement are two affordable alternatives. Some compatibility issues with InDesign have been reported in the editing community in regard to PDF-XChange. It's not compatible with a Mac either. PDFelement works with Mac OS and Windows.

Compressing PDFs

If budget is an issue, there are free online PDF-compression tools that reduce file size. I've tested Soda PDF but a Google Search will give you many more options.

Creating branded cover pages

Add a branded cover page to your file. It bulks up the file size but reassures the reader that they've downloaded the correct product, and makes your written content look more attractive.

If you're uploading a book/guide file to Amazon KDP, the cover should be omitted. Note also that Amazon requires PDFs for print-book covers.

Working with Amazon KDP

Offering written content via Amazon KDP is relatively straightforward. There are good quality-control steps in place to allow you to check your proofs prior to publication, and if you discover a gremlin further down the line you can update the content.

Be sure to read Amazon's guidelines carefully. In the Resources section, there's a link to its guidance on formatting a manuscript and creating covers for ebooks and paperbacks (see Amazon KDP publishing resources).

Edit and be edited

This goes without saying but do take your PIP through the editing process. Is perfection possible? Of course not, just as we all know from our client work. But several rounds of self-editing and a final quality-control check by a trusted colleague will keep standards up and stress down. I know from experience that the job I do and the audience of writers and editors I create content for add to the pressure. Investing in the services of someone I trust is a no-brainer.

Creating video content

Video is a powerful tool because at the very least it allows people to hear your voice, and perhaps even your face. That's engaging. It also means they can multitask. Several students have told me they enjoyed being able to do a first run-through of my course content by *listening* to the webinar while they were doing something else.

Furthermore, some types of content work best when students can *see* what they need to do (e.g. tutorials of how to do something technical). Visual representations of key concepts can also aid comprehension.

However, video content isn't always the most accessible option when people are on the go, so do create a written version of the core learning too. It respects your customers' busy lifestyles and different preferences. Plus, you might consider repurposing it as an additional standalone PIP for those on a budget.

Recording video

Here are three tools that will enable you to create slide-based webinars, face-to-camera videos, and tutorials.

- I recommend turning a slide deck into a webinar with Microsoft 365's PowerPoint. Use the save-as function and choose 'MPEG-Video' from the dropdown menu.
- For face-to-camera work, your inbuilt or plugin webcam might be good enough quality. Otherwise, use your smart phone to record a short introductory webinar and then move to PowerPoint for the slide-deck work.
- Snagit is a reasonably priced tool that offers screen-casting functionality. Great for tutorials and demonstrations. Zoom is completely free and does a fabulous job too.

Adding audio

The reason I use PowerPoint to create videos for slide-based course materials is that audio is so simple to add.

- You'll need a headset with a mic. I use Microsoft's LifeChat LX 6000, which costs around £30.
- Audio can be added on a slide-by-slide basis, which means if you stumble you need only rerecord one slide, not the whole module.
- Head for the Insert tab, click on the small arrow under the Audio symbol, and choose Record Audio. A window will pop up. Press the red button to start recording, and the square when you're finished. Then drag the icon into the space outside of your slide.
- Use the Transitions tab to choose different effects (e.g. fade) from one slide to the next.
- Still in the Transitions tab, go the Advance Slide settings and place a tick in the After checkbox. Left-click on the

audio icon you moved off-slide. Now left-click on the bar to the right of the arrow. Drag your cursor as far to the right as you can. A time-stamp will show up.

- Head back up to the Advance Slide settings and edit the time-stamp there. That will ensure that the slide won't transition in your final video until after you've finished speaking.

Editing video

For most of us, editing means nothing more fancy than being able to remove the bits where we stumble or cough or the dog walks in.

- Basic cuts can be done in YouTube.
- If you have an iOS device, the iMovie app will let you do the job with one finger. It's easy to create gentle transitions between your edits, too.
- If you have an Android device, try PowerDirector. The functionality is similar to iMovie's.
- If you have the budget, Camtasia is a paid-for video-editing and creation suite that comes highly recommended. If you already have it, great – use it. If not, think hard about whether the investment is worth it – try the free tools first.

Compressing large video files

If you do decide to upload video files direct to your website, bear in mind that they're bulky. This means upload times are longer, valuable space is taken up on your computer, and the load time on your website could be slower (which the search engines don't like).

- Download Handbrake – it's free, safe, and will shrink your videos with imperceptible loss in quality.

Adding closed captions/subtitles

A whopping 85% of videos are played with the sound off. Creating subtitles/captions for your videos is therefore recommended. It respects people who are hard-of-hearing and those with different preferences. You can create subtitles for free in YouTube or pay a small fee to Rev.

Hosting video

Video is greedy and will slow down your website if it's uploaded direct (or natively). I therefore recommend hosting on a dedicated platform if you want to deliver your PIP on your website. That way, the platform, not your website, bears the load. The two best-known platforms are Vimeo and YouTube.

Set your video's visibility settings in YouTube to Unlisted. That means your paid-for content won't be available to anyone but those who have access to the private page on your website or who've been given the video's URL.

Embed the content in your website using the using the embed-code tool.

- Go to your video on your YouTube account, click on the title, select the SHARE button, and click on the EMBED button.
- Grab the code that appears in the new window. Open your website's embed-code tool and paste the html code you copied from YouTube. The code will look something like this:

  <iframe width= "560" height="315" src="https://www.youtube.com/embed/XX XXXXXXX?rel=0" frameborder="0" allow="autoplay; encrypted-media" allowfullscreen></iframe>

- Amend the width and height to suit your own display preferences.
- Use Aspect Ratio Calculator to change the size of a video without losing the proportions.

Creating audio content

Audio content is hugely popular, and while I wouldn't recommend offering it exclusively for most PIPs, it's a fantastic supplement to consider because it offers a hands- and screen-free content experience.

Audiobooks

Creating audiobooks is demanding, and not to be taken lightly.

The big decision is whether to do it yourself or commission a professional voice artist. Doing it yourself adds masses of value because you're literally bringing your brand voice to the product – and that's a powerful engagement tool. It's much cheaper too.

However, there's a big learning curve for the newbie, and you'll need the right environment and high-quality kit.

- Professional voice artist Ray Greenley offers comprehensive advice in this free booklet: *Audio-book Production: A Primer for Indie Authors*.
- John Espirian shares his experience of turning *Content DNA* into an audiobook in this blog article: 'Audiobook production'.
- Joanna Penn's book *Audio for Authors* explores various aspects of audio content, from podcasting to audiobook creation. Naturally, there's an audiobook version if you'd prefer to listen to Penn than to read her words.
- The primary marketplace for producing audiobooks is ACX. Audible is the most well-known distributor. Both are owned by Amazon.
- Avoid recording spaces with echo. If you have a small room or closet space, hang a soft lining like a blanket or sheet around the interior walls to absorb the noise.

Short-form bonus audio content

If the costs and production time required for creating audiobooks feel onerous, might there be space for an audio version of shorter-form content?

For example, let's say you include a short ebook as part of a multimedia course. An audio version that complements the webinar and book, and which you pitch as a bonus rather than a standalone product with its own price tag, would not require expensive narration and hosting costs. Plus, because it's a bonus, your audience will be a little more forgiving if you're new to audiocasting.

Recording and editing tools

Which tools you'll need will depend on what you're doing.

For recording and editing any form of audio content, Audacity is a superb free tool that you can record straight into and edit with. Denise Cowle and I use it for The Editing Podcast. Ray Greenley, the pro voice artist I mentioned above, uses it for audiobook production.

As for which mic to go with, it's a personal choice because what works with your voice might not work for someone else's. If you're going down the audiobook route, Blue, Shure and RØDE are respected brands, but they're not cheap. For shorter-form bonus content, you might well be able to get away with something like the Microsoft headset I've already mentioned.

Environment is a critical factor when it comes to quality. With bonus audio material, your audience will forgive a squeaky chair. With standalone audio content that costs the customer money, that won't be acceptable and will fail the submission standards required by a production/distribution channel such as ACX.

Other recording tools for bonus content include Cleanfeed, Skype and Zoom, all of which have free versions.

Hosting and distribution

ACX and Audible are the go-to platforms for hosting and distribution of audio books. Take care to investigate the contract terms so you know how long you're tied in for.

For those wishing to embed shorter-form audio content on private website pages, SoundCloud is an excellent audio streaming platform that offers a restricted number of free uploads.

Native audio uploads are less bulky than video, so this could be another option if your website has the necessary plugin.

If you plan to create audio regularly, Captivate and Libsyn are podcasting hosts that offer affordable monthly plans. Just bear in mind that if you stop paying the subscription, your content could disappear. Make sure you keep the original files so you can upload natively to your website later if you wish.

Design and branding tools

A PIP should look as though it's come out of your stable. That doesn't mean all your PIPs must look identical. Think in terms of themes or elements that tie products to your editing business:

- Your logo
- Your colour palette
- The fonts you use
- Images

I have two guide series: Transform Your Fiction and Business Skills for Editors. Each series has distinct artwork, but the images for both were created by the same artist with my editorial brand palette in mind. My standalone books are different colours but the font and logo used for each are identical.

Canva is my top recommendation for design. Even the free version is knockout. The onboard templates mean even those with no design experience can create lovely branded artwork for their business.

Should you hire a pro? It depends on your skills, your time, how complex your intended design is, and your budget. I commissioned a professional designer to create my series artwork because I could offset the cost against multiple guides, but did the job myself for the standalone books and multimedia courses.

Stepping outside the comfort zone

Editors are used to charging for their editing services. We're confident in our skills. Creating a paid-for product that will generate passive income can feel like a step into a very uncomfortable place, especially because there may be new skills to learn and new ways of communicating our knowledge.

I understand that – I've been through it. I still go through it every time I bring a new product to market. It's as if I've forgotten the day I sent back my first ever editing job, the first day I published a blog post, the first day I stood up in a room and presented to an audience.

Fear is normal. Parts of the learning curve appear insurmountable at first glance. But they're not, I promise you. Many of the skills and tools you need to create your PIP are ones you already have. The others can be learned.

FOR YOU TO DO

Access your planner and go to the section on **creation tools**. Record your ideas about the following:

- What tools do you need to bring your PIP to life? Do you already have them, or will you need to invest?
- Do you know how to use all those tools? If not, will you learn or hire a specialist to do the work for you?
- Research any tutorials you need to assist you with the work. YouTube and Google Search are awash with useful free

guidance. Make a note of the URLs so you can return to that guidance when you're ready.

- Make a list of associated costs for editing, artwork, audio and video creation.

Stage 5: Promotion and visibility

Now it's time to think about the steps you'll take to put your PIP in front of its audience – the promotion plan. I'm going to offer you a range of solutions. Pick and choose what will work best for your product type.

Promotional format

For each type of promotion there will be multiple ways in which you can format your promotional message. Even within a single campaign you can use different types of content (e.g. a blog article with a video or image).

Written content

This is the preferred option for many an editor because we're in our comfort zone! Examples include:

- Blog posts
- Press releases
- Articles for industry magazines, newsletters and journals
- LinkedIn and Facebook posts
- Website copy for dedicated PIP pages

Video

The least favourite option for many an editor because we're way out of our comfort zone! Some of the options I've listed here are less intimidating than others.

- Recorded face-to-camera work
- Live face-to-camera work
- Sample excerpts from PIP webinars

- Videos made with still images. Design in Canva. Upload to a tool such as MoShow
- Gifs. Create the images in Canva. Create with a tool such as Giphy
- Tutorials about how to install or use tool-based PIPs

Audio

Audio is big and getting bigger. It's great for engaging with an audience in a way that's rich with your personality but avoids face-to-camera jitters.

- Narrate sample chapters. Record into Audacity, Skype or Zoom
- Record shorter audio promo – audiograms – and create audiograms with Headliner
- Repurpose video promo content with Headliner to create audio-only (or create videograms with audio-only content)

Images

Supplement written content about your PIP with engaging images that draw the eye. Use a tool like Canva, which has thousands of beautiful templates to draw on. Examples include:

- Infographics
- Screenshots from a PIP webinar
- Cover-design artwork
- Social media images
- Blog post header images

Type of promotion

I recommend doing several different types of promotion because not all marketing is the same. Some activities get you in front of a target audience immediately but the impact is short-lived. Some strategies are a slow burn but the impact is long-lasting. Furthermore, the type of content customers respond to most positively varies from person to person. Here are some options for you to consider.

Paid online advertising

Paid ads have a fast impact but last only as long as the promotion runs, which will be determined by how much you invest.

If you have experience of targeted online advertising and know how to get a product or service in front of the right audience, go for it. If you don't, tread carefully and think about consulting with a marketing pro. For example, there's little point in carrying out a Facebook ads campaign if you haven't installed a Facebook pixel on your website.

Ideas to try

- Facebook ads – you'll need to master Facebook's Ads Manager. Even pro marketers acknowledge that there's a learning curve.
- Google ads.
- If the target audience is fellow editors, and if you're a member of a national editorial society, find out whether you can pay to target the membership.

Social media promotion

Focus on the platforms where your target audience is hanging out. For you that might be Facebook; for someone else it might be Instagram, LinkedIn or Twitter.

If you're already connected with your core audience on social media, and have lots of followers, placing notices about your PIP launch into your feeds will get people's attention quickly. If you're a social media newbie, the impact will be slower.

Some feeds are faster and noisier than others. Blink and a target customer might miss your notification on Twitter. It's therefore worth thinking about promotion strategies that are more likely to get you noticed on social media so that you receive the all-important organic-reach boost from the algorithms without paying a penny. Spammy hard sells on your Facebook business page are far less likely to be effective than fun promotions such as chatbot commenting campaigns.

Ideas to try

- If the target audience for your PIP is the editorial community, the EAE Ad Space is an Editors' Association of Earth offshoot group that welcomes free advertising from our community. Knock yourself out and promote your PIP without shame!
- Post written announcements on your LinkedIn feed. Words work well with LinkedIn!
- On Facebook, video is king. Post videos on your business page feed. Upload directly rather than linking; the algorithms prefer it so you'll get better organic reach.
- Create a Twitter thread with images, chapter headings and short summaries.
- Create a chatbot commenting campaign on your Facebook page – see 'Chatbot commenting campaign' in the Resources section.
- Create a gif countdown campaign on your Facebook page or via your blog, in which you offer a free copy of your PIP to one viewer who comments during the period of the campaign. Place the entrants' names into Wheel of Names and record your screen as you select the winner. Post the video live on social media.
- Share a narrated audio sample of your PIP on social media.

Content marketing

Content marketing is a slow burn but the benefits are long-lasting. Blog posts, vlogs and podcast episodes can be shared over and over so think about related *free* content you can create that positions you as an expert in the field of your PIP – someone who understands and is capable of addressing and solving problems. That's the best way to put yourself top of mind when people are searching for solutions.

Content marketing is about earning trust. Customers (including clients and colleagues) are more likely to part with their cash for a deeper-dive paid-for product if they love what you're offering with your freebies.

Ideas to try

- Guest on a relevant podcast. Ask for your PIP to be included in the show notes.
- Pitch a guest post for a relevant influencer's blog – include a link to your PIP in your bio.
- Write blog posts about related problems. Refer and link to the PIP gently – framing it as a deeper dive – either at the end of the post in a related-resources section or within the post if appropriate.
- Create tutorials about related problems.
- Include a list of related resources on the back page of free booklets and other downloadable content available on your site.
- Create a learning zone or resource hub on your website that pulls in or links to your free content.

Email marketing

Perhaps the mention of email marketing sets off your spam alert. I get it. But I'm not suggesting you buy in a mailing list. Rather, I recommend building your own. That means your mailouts are targeted at your existing fanbase. That's where the power lies.

People who bother to sign up are telling you they're interested in what you're doing, so much so that they're prepared to give you one of the most valuable pieces of data they possess – their email address. It's a strong demonstration of their trust.

Email marketing is a longer-haul enterprise because the email list has to be built. And only if you have something to share regularly will people bother subscribing. Content marketing and social media engagement are therefore central to the strategy.

In terms of the immediacy of impact, email marketing is a little more complex. Yes, the life of the campaign is only as long as the email sits in someone's inbox, but if there is other useful free content in your newsletter, it might not be deleted after the first reading.

Furthermore, with email marketing you commit to sending your newsletter regularly. I send mine once a month. Others do weekly mailouts. It's about trying to get a balance that keeps your subscribers informed regularly enough that they don't forget who you are but not so regularly that they consider your emails as inbox-cloggers.

In the main, use your newsletter to inform, share and give. If you do that, no one will mind a few links to paid-for content that adds value and solves problems.

Ideas to try

- Trial MailChimp's free option. You won't pay a penny until you've reached 2,000 subscribers.
- Use MailChimp's free Landing Page tool to create pre-launch sign-ups for people who want to register their interest. Place sign-up buttons on the PIP page on your website. When you launch, you'll have a highly targeted list of people who want to hear from you and buy from you.
- Place any links to paid-for content at the bottom of your regular newsletter mailouts. All the free goodies – resources, tools, blog posts etc. – should come first.
- If selling via email marketing makes you nervous, frame the information about your PIP in terms of news. Focus

on the goals and outcomes of the PIP rather than your endeavour.

- Customize your email signature to include your PIP.
- Give a narrated audio sample of a book to your subscribers.

Website marketing

This is passive promotion because it involves no participation on your part other than making information available.

Listings are valuable because they last for as long as you keep the content up, and you control the space and the message. However, impact relies on the customer visiting your website in the first place, so the response is unlikely to be immediate unless your site is already top of mind for many of your target customers. That's where content marketing and customizable directory listings can help.

The most valuable real estate on your website is near the top. Most websites have tabs that take visitors to different spaces – home page, contact page, services page. Make sure you have a tab for your PIPs. For example, I have Training and Books tabs.

Ideas to try

- Create a resource library or learning zone and include your PIP.
- Add a linked image, video or audiogram into the sidebar of your blog.
- List your PIP in a Tools and Publications section on your bio and qualifications pages.
- Source product testimonials and place them on the PIP's page.
- Add Amazon Associates links to any books and guides you've published there.
- Place a narrated audio sample on the PIP's page.

Community and convention marketing

This includes slower-burn activities such as being active in editorial and client-side networks and online forums, and shorter-lived but faster-impact activities like convention promotion.

Ideas to try

- Customize your forum signature such that it links to your PIP.
- Present a seminar or workshop at a convention around the subject matter of your PIP. Give the PIP to the delegates for free or at a discount.
- Place fliers in conference packs.
- Offer your PIP as a raffle prize.
- Host a free draw in which your PIP is the prize.
- Post an announcement in EAE Ad Space if relevant to your target audience.
- Request a book-signing slot at a convention.

Directory advertising

If your directory listings allow it, link not only to free resources that demonstrate your expertise but also to your PIP. Of course, the focus should be on your editorial services if that's the purpose of your advertising there in the first place, but a well-placed video or click-through image can generate targeted leads to relevant products.

Ideas to try

- CIEP members can customize their entries in the Chartered Institute of Editing and Proofreading (CIEP) Directory of Editorial Services.
- Find a Proofreader and Freelancers in the UK allow external links.
- Include images and short videos if allowed.

Retail outlets

This is another form of passive marketing. If your PIP's a book or guide, you'd be bonkers not to make it available for sale on Amazon – the biggest store on the planet.

Still, those platforms are crowded, and even though your books and guides will be serving niche audiences, users might not know who you are. Impact is likely to be slower and driven in the longer term by engagement with your target audience in other spaces.

Ideas to try

- Start with Amazon KDP.
- Consider going wide with Ingram Spark and Smashwords.
- Ask local libraries if they'll stock your book.
- Present yourself to bookstores as a local author.

Promotion schedule

Think about your pre- and post-launch promotion strategy. You don't need to wait until the product's available to start telling people about it.

Soft pre-launches can take the form of announcements in newsletter mailouts, references in related blog posts, register-your-interest buttons on your website, gif countdowns on social media, and Wheel of Names free draws.

Creating a schedule enables you to organize your PIP promotion campaign without feeling overwhelmed.

FOR YOU TO DO

Access your planner and go to the section on **promotion and visibility**. Record your ideas about the following:

- What formats you will use for promotion.
- Which combinations of the different types of promotion will get your PIP in front of your target audience.
- Any costs you'll incur.
- What you'll need to learn in order to carry out some types of promotion.
- The schedule for pre-and post-launch campaigns.

Beating impostor syndrome

Maybe you're thinking, 'No way, not me. How can I create a product and ask people to pay for it?' If so, impostor syndrome has knocked on the door. This short chapter aims to help you send it on its merry way.

What the impostor voice sounds like

The impostor voice tells us we're not good enough, that we have no right to create this product, that people will think we're daft, that the product will be no good, that we don't know enough, aren't special enough. Of course, none of these things are true, and editors know it. Still, we're a sensitive bunch and prone to allowing fear to hold us back.

Ideas for how to deal with impostor syndrome

Familiarize yourself

The first thing to do is recognize it. Doing so makes that voice more familiar, and that alone can reduce its power a little. It's less of a shock, though no less vindictive.

Consider whether there are triggers that are likely to make the voice louder and stop you developing a passive income stream. Understanding when the voice is loudest can help us ready ourselves to quieten it down before it becomes deafening. Perhaps there are particular times of day, month or year when you're more prone to being anxious, either for business or personal reasons. Maybe you have a recurring gig with a particular client that's a stress point. It might even be a setting that induces negative thoughts.

If you can identify spaces and times when you're *less* likely to be plagued by impostor syndrome, that's the time to plan your PIP.

Focus on the problem/solution premise

Think back to the core characteristics of a PIP, and Stage 1 of the PIP Development Framework. If you've identified problems and come up with solutions, you've demonstrated your right to deliver assistance in whichever form you choose. That's where the truth lies – in the expertise that enables you to offer solutions to problems – not in the negative voice in your head.

Get support

Get your PIP checked by pros you trust. That'll help affirm the quality. I even get my free blog content checked by a colleague to allay my fears.

Talk through your PIP with a colleague you trust and respect. Use *them* as the sounding board for your fears so that the messaging for the public is positive. Remember, you're solving problems. That needs to have a confident message even if the impostor voice is poking you in the arm and shouting in your ear.

Acknowledge the learning process

It's likely that youll do research to fill in knowledge or skills gaps. That can help to frame the creation of a PIP as a form of continued professional development. Most editors I know love learning and are proud of that. Make passive income generation a part of that journey.

Frame it in terms of client mindfulness

It can help to think about clients when negative thoughts settle in. Many of them experience anxiety when they put their books and articles in front of an editor, especially the first time. Experiencing those feelings ourselves puts us on their side of the fence. We can learn from that experience, and improve our mindfulness when communicating with them.

Accept that you're nervous

It's normal to be nervous. Feeling anxious is not the same thing as having an anxiety disorder. If your fear comes from the former, acknowledge the feeling rather than trying to push it away. It's about letting it sit at the table, but not at the *head* of that table. If the impostor voice speaks too loudly, try quietening it with breathing exercises.

Respond to the impostor with your best defence

Imagine the impostor has written you a letter. Write down their criticisms. Then respond to them with a counterargument that demonstrates why they're mistaken. Use the PIP planner to remind yourself of everything you know, the problems you can solve, the new skills you'll develop, and the planning you've done.

Then head to your website and look at your logo. It's a visual reminder that you're a professional editor who runs their own business. And business owners earn income – passively and actively.

Do it anyway

You're not alone. I suffer from impostor syndrome. I so wish someone had invented ImpostorBuster just like in our Stage 2 case study! Create your PIP anyway. No one will know you're nervous unless you tell them. And why would you when you have a much more important thing to offer – a solution to their problems.

I look forward to seeing what you come up with.

Louise

Resources

Adobe Reader DC: Free PDF editor

Amazon KDP publishing resources

Aspect Ratio Calculator: Image resizing and proportion-retaining tool

Audacity: Free, open-source audio recording and editing software

Audio for Authors: Book, Joanna Penn, Curl Up Press, 2020

Audiobook production: Article, John Espirian

Audio-book Production: Booklet, Ray Greenley

Blogging for Business Growth: Online multimedia course, Louise Harnby

Boxshot Lite: 3D-image creation – perfect for booklets

Business Planning for Editorial Freelancers: Book, Louise Harnby, Panx Press, 2013

Camtasia: Screen recorder and video editor

Canva: Free graphic design tool

Chatbot commenting campaign: 'How to market your book and build your author platform using a chatbot': Article by Louise Harnby, The Editing Blog

Cleanfeed: Browser-based audio recording tool

Content DNA: Book, John Espirian, 2020

EAE Ad Space: Facebook group

Editing Fiction at Sentence Level: Book, Louise Harnby, Panx Press, 2020

Find a Proofreader: Open editing directory

Giphy: Free gif-maker

Google Slides: Free document creation and design tool

Handbrake: Video compression tool

Headliner: Free tool for creating audiograms, video autograms and video transcripts

Hotmart: Ecommerce platform (courses)

How not to be a LinkedIn Loser: Article, John Espirian

How to Build an Editorial Blog: Book, Louise Harnby, Panx Press, 2020

How to Create an Ebook in Canva: Article, Andrew and Pete

How to do Content Marketing: Book, Louise Harnby, Panx Press, 2020 (formerly *Content Marketing Primer*, 2017)

How to Write the Perfect Fiction Editorial Report: Online multimedia course, Louise Harnby

Lumen5: Free video creation tool

MailChimp: Email marketing and blog-post distribution tool

Marketing Your Editing & Proofreading Business: Book, Louise Harnby, Panx Press, 2014

MoShow: Video creation app available via Google Apps and Apple stores

Omnibus: Editorial Business Planning and Marketing: Book, Louise Harnby, Panx Press, 2016

Payhip: Ecommerce platform (digital products and memberships)

PDFelement: PDF editor

PDF-XChange: PDF editor

Pixabay: Royalty-free images

Podia: Ecommerce platform (digital products and memberships)

PowerDirector: Android video-editing app

Pricing a Project: How to prepare a professional quotation: Guide, Melanie Thompson, CIEP

Proofreading Theses and Dissertations: Guide, Stephen Cashmore, CIEP

Proofreading Theses and Dissertations: Online course, CIEP

Rev: Transcription, captioning and subtitling service

Sellfy: Ecommerce platform (digital products and subscriptions)

Skype: Online audio and video conferencing tool with recording capability

Snagit: Snipping, screencasting and image-annotation tool

Social Media for Business Growth: Online multimedia course, Louise Harnby

SoundCloud: Audio hosting service

Switching to Fiction: Online multimedia course, Louise Harnby

Tea and Commas: The Foundations of Line and Copy-Editing Fiction: Online course, Sophie Playle

TinyPNG: Image compressor

Udemy: Ecommerce platform (courses)

Unsplash: Royalty-free images

Wheel of Names: Online random-selection tool

Writing a content-marketing book. With John Espirian: The Editing
    Podcast S4E3
Yellowpipe: Brand-colour converter (hex and RGB)
Zoom: Online audio and video conferencing tool with recording
    capability

The PIP planner

SCHEDULE	
When will you develop your PIP?	

PROBLEMS, SKILLS AND SOLUTIONS	
What you know #1: Editing skills	
What you know #2: Niche specialisms	

What you know #3:	
Business skills	

What you know #4:	
Background knowledge	

The problems you regularly solve #1:	
In client work	

The problems you regularly solve #2:	
In networking and training spaces	
The problems you regularly solve #3:	
In your head	
The problems you regularly solve #4:	
In your business	

Solutions that can be PIPs #1: Solutions exist – you bring a new angle and position yourself as an expert	
Solutions that can be PIPs #2: Partial solutions exist – you bring niche approaches and/or new formats	
Solutions that can be PIPs #3: No solutions exist – you offer one	

What content have you already created #1? Conventions/workshops	
What content have you already created #2? Training experience	
What content have you already created #3? Written or audiovisual (e.g. blog posts, guest blog posts, podcast guesting, interviews, articles for magazines and newsletters)	

AUDIENCE	
Who is the audience?	
Where is the audience?	
How high is trust?	

How will you maintain and build trust?	
SHAPE	
Outline the type of product and its components (e.g. course with video and book, video and checklist):	

Scaling opportunities:	
Format (e.g. print, MOBI, webinar, audio, code):	
How will customers access the PIP (e.g. website, third party, retail outlet):	

Payment systems:	
CREATION TOOLS	
What tools do you have or need?	
Which tools require you to upskill?	

Tutorial links:	
Costs:	
Existing skills:	

PROMOTION AND VISIBILITY	
Formats (e.g. written, video):	
Types of promotion you'll carry out (e.g. content marketing, website marketing, social media):	
Costs of promotion:	

Skills you need to learn and URLs for resources that will assist you:	
Promotion schedule #1: Pre-launch	

Promotion schedule #2: Post-launch	

Printed in Great Britain
by Amazon